leadership
on the
level

JERRY MEEK

Praise for *Leadership on the Level*

"My wife and I met Jerry and his Desert Star team through referrals, people that had done business with Desert Star for an extended period of time. The project I wanted to build was unique and I was certain it would take a team of people with vision and commitment to actually get it across the finish line. Jerry and his team certainly have that and more.

"Jerry is a man of faith and it is evident in many ways. His eyes are that of a 5-year-old, excited and can't wait to see what life has in store for him each day. The team Jerry has put together is a big part of the 'magic sauce' for his success. The approach he uses empowers people to think and take ownership of their work, resulting in leaders who will get the job done. The Meeks have a genuine interest and relationship with their team and their customers. They are exceptional people, and it is a pleasure for my wife and I to call them friends."

—LARRY VAN TUYL, CEO of Van Tuyl Group
Former Chairman Berkshire Hathaway Automotive

"*Leadership on the Level* will restore balance in your life as a leader and inspire your team to new heights. Jerry Meek knows that the best leaders follow the example of Jesus and serve others with strength, humility, and compassion. Drawing on the wisdom of the Beatitudes and Jerry's years of dynamic leadership in construction, this book is an essential toolbox for advancing God's Kingdom."

—CHRIS HODGES, Senior Pastor, Church of the Highlands
Author of *The Daniel Dilemma* and *Out of the Cave*

"Reading *Leadership on the Level* comes at the right time as I am about to embark on a new senior leadership journey with a top tech company. Modeling my leadership after Jesus has always a priority. Jerry's authenticity, humility, and willingness to share successes and failures are inspiring. I will take many of the learnings from the book to ensure I am hiring the right people, setting the right vision, taking care of customers, and creating the best culture for my organization. This is a must read!"

—CHERRYL PRESSLEY, Former Senior Director
Microsoft Corporation

"'Successful people never lose sight of their mission.' In *Leadership on the Level*, Jerry Meek does a remarkable job of inter weaving business leadership and Christian principles. Jerry masterfully ties together everyday examples of how to lead your team and then draws the parallel to how Jesus led his team. The book was both encouraging and thought provoking. I personally am inspired to lead by being the salt and light in my own company."

—MARC POORTINGA, President/CEO
   Distinctive Cabinetry

"My family has worked with the Jerry Meek for over forty years, and each one of us should strive toward their level of dedication, honesty, and selflessness. This book should serve as an inspiration to all who are deeply entrenched in operating a business of any kind. Jerry's words are a wonderful reminder of the importance of making the people around you a part of your success story and realizing that none of us can do it alone. I plan to read and re-read and share *Leadership on the Level* as much as I possibly can. It truly inspires to be the best you can be."

—SARAH HILDEBRANDT, President
   Clyde Hardware Co., Inc.

"For well over a decade, I have watched Jerry apply the lessons recorded in *Leadership on The Level* in real time, in real life. Such practical insights from an incredibly humble leader."

—BEN LENTZ, Founder and CEO
Cyber Technology Group

"There's no greater example of life-changing leadership than Christ. From His prayerful selection of leaders, to the empowerment of those who would carry out His eternal mission, He is still the ideal example of leadership. In his new book, Jerry has identified and unpacked brilliant leadership concepts from Christ's example from the Sermon on the Mount. Through the lenses of Scripture and his inspiring personal journey, Jerry will give you new insight and applicable steps on how to achieve a greater level of leadership now and leave a legacy of leadership for others to follow."

—BLAKE HAMON, Campus Pastor, Free Chapel Braselton

"Jerry offers a most compelling and transparent view into his interpersonal leadership style by presenting them on a backdrop of the Beatitudes, or the Beautiful Attitudes, as he describes them. *Leadership on the Level* shares insight through personal stories and profound scriptural references, not only as relatable verses, but exactly as the Jerry has chosen to lead his business. This is not a step by step, how-to book, it's much more! One will learn valuable Biblical lessons which are applicable in every industry and more importantly, in all relationships. Jerry truly takes leadership to a new level!"

—MICHAEL OSBORNE, Founder and Chairman
Mammoth Tech

"For over three decades I have watched Jerry Meek build a great brand, organization, reputation, and relationships. *Leadership on The Level* is a book that will show you how Desert Star Construction became successful. Each page reveals time-tested biblical truths. A must read for those seeking to accomplish more than the norm."

—DAVID CAVAN, Founder and Chairman
Cavan Companies

leadership
on the
level

JERRY MEEK

FOREWORD BY DR. DARRYN SCHESKE

HIGH BRIDGE BOOKS
HOUSTON

Leadership on the Level
by Jerry Meek

High Bridge Books titles may be purchased in bulk for educational, business, fundraising, or sales promotional use. For information, please contact High Bridge Books via www.HighBridgeBooks.com/contact.

Published in Houston, Texas by High Bridge Books.

Also by Jerry Meek

*While You Wait: Finding
Purpose in the "Not Yets"*

Be Great...Before It's Too Late

*Teambuilder Toolbox: 13 Tools to
Build the Power of Your Team*

Dedication

Do you want to be better tomorrow than you are today? Do you desire to make a lasting, positive impact on your family, through your work, and in your community? Are you wondering how you can shine your light a little brighter each day?

Whether you are just beginning your chosen endeavor or have already reached a high level of success, this book is dedicated to you, the one who acts. The lifelong learner who doesn't just read books on leadership but prayerfully applies the lessons they learn to make a difference in their world.

Contents

Foreword _____ xvii

Preface _____ xxiii

Introduction _____ xxvii

1. On the Level _____ 1

2. A Bit of (Head-Scratching) History _____ 5

3. Climbing the Mountain _____ 13

4. Calling Your Team _____ 23

5. The Anatomy of a Team _____ 31

6. Empowering Your Team _____ 39

7. The Beautiful Attitudes _____ 47

8. Blessed Are the Poor _____ 53

9. Blessed Are the Hungry _____ 63

10. Blessed Are the Brokenhearted _____ 71

11. Blessed Are the Rejected _____ 81

12. Salt and Light _____ 89

13. What About Judas? _____ 97

Acknowledgements _____ 105

References _____ 107

Suggested Reading _____ 109

Join the Glorious Reflections Community _____ 115

Take the Challenge: 21 Days to Living and Leading in
   a Way That Reflects the Glory of God _____ 117

About the Author _____ 119

Foreword

I first met Jerry Meek at a Kingdom Builders Summit in Colorado. Kingdom Builders was founded by entrepreneur-turned-pastor, Lee Domingue, and the Summit is a gathering designed to refresh and re-envision pastors and business leaders about the unique calling they have in each other's lives. Jerry and his wife, Carol, were featured speakers at the Summit, invited to share the story of how they founded their custom home building company, Desert Star Construction.

Listening to Jerry and Carol speak, I knew they were smart. They had built a company where the combined annual sales revenue of their clients is in excess of $4 trillion dollars and growing. But the more they spoke, the more I was captivated by their humility.

They spoke of the many lessons they had learned from their mistakes, the struggles in their marriage, and the tragedies they had experienced along the way. I immediately sensed their deep love for God and people and their childlike joy in accelerating the building of God's Kingdom through their generosity.

I was so impressed by their story. Early the next morning, I downloaded Jerry's book *Be Great...Before It's Too Late* and devoured the entire thing before breakfast. I learned that in 2008, when the national housing crisis caused the construction market to collapse, Jerry's homebuilding company lost $25 million worth of work over a forty-five-day period. Jerry sat down with his team and told them, "We are not going to participate in the recession." He told them that he and Carol would not take a paycheck until the economy turned around and that no one would be laid off. He said, "Rather than hunker down, we did the opposite. We took the opportunity to invest in our team..."

As I took the elevator down to the hotel lobby, I marveled over this incredible perspective. When the doors opened, Jerry himself was standing there. I told him how much I enjoyed reading his book, and he invited me to breakfast. Neither of us knew that the next few hours would launch such an incredible friendship and mentoring relationship. I asked many questions that morning about his decision to invest in his team. Over and over, Jerry reiterated that no one accomplishes anything great alone. Jerry doesn't just hire employees—he elevates everyone around him!

My wife and I moved to Indianapolis and started our church in our home on the first Sunday of February in 2001. Amongst our first members were our real estate broker, our mortgage broker, and our homeowners insurance agent—the only people we knew in the city. In total, there were seventeen people (that's including all of our kids!).

Our mortgage broker and our homeowners insurance agent were among the first of eighty-nine people who publicly proclaimed their new faith in Christ through baptism that first year.

As the church grew in size, so did our leadership problems and dilemmas. I thought I had to have all the answers, and I quickly discovered how little I really knew.

Thankfully, I didn't do ministry alone. I was a part of the Converge church planting movement and had a seasoned church planter named Gary Rohrmayer for a coach. He gave me the book, *Spiritual Leadership* by Henry and Richard Blackaby, and the principles in that book changed my life.

I discovered that others knew much more about leadership than I did, and I began seeking out leaders who could teach me what they knew. To this day, I am grateful for those who poured their wisdom into me—they've helped us build our church and make an impact in our city, nation, and world.

I now have the honor of serving as Chairman of Converge, a network of over 1,300 churches across America. Together we are starting and strengthening life-giving churches across the country. In every case where a church is growing, we find that leaders are growing. It's *always* about leadership.

That's where *Leadership on the Level* comes in. This is not another how-to book with seven sure-fire steps to becoming a better leader. Rather, this book relays the wisdom Jerry's amassed over the years through starting a successful construction company with his father out of the bed of a pickup truck where the plans for their first home-building project were on a single sheet of paper.

Jerry's is a story less about building homes and more about the importance of building relationships, though it would be a mistake to think that he sacrifices excellence.

The successes Jerry and Desert Star have experienced come from a relationally-based process where trust is built to the point where each team member can level with each other.

Jerry is gifted in his ability to listen and ask thoughtful (sometimes piercing) questions, but he listens in a way that encourages you to talk more. Of all the leaders I've met, he is one of the best I know at building trust with those around him. He's been building his team for decades, some of whom have been with him for over twenty years.

If you want to be a better leader, read this book! Learn from Jerry's examples and what God has taught him through his personal and professional life. In short, let him level with you. Ponder his questions. Consider the wisdom he imparts from scripture. And put these principles into practice in your life. You will not be disappointed with the results. By the end of this book, I know you will understand the truth in the title, *Leadership on the Level.*

—Dr. Darryn L. Scheske
    Senior Pastor
    Heartland Church
    Indianapolis, Indiana

Preface

I've been in construction all my life. My father had me on jobsites with him when I was five years old. While I've certainly learned what I am capable of, over forty years in the business has also taught me a lot about my limitations.

What started as a two-man team that provided rough and finish carpentry for commercial buildings and custom residential homes has grown into what is now Desert Star Construction, our custom home building company that in 2019 had an annual revenue of nearly $50 million with over $150 million of work in progress.

Most of our clients are leaders in their respective industries (technology, aerospace, cybersecurity, microchip manufacturing, retail, professional athletes, and more). We were even blessed with the opportunity to build two homes for George Trimble, the first man in history to appear before Congress and secure a billion dollars in funding for NASA. (He oversaw all the Apollo missions through 14 and even invented the "T" tail you see on modern airplanes.)

Though we now have the opportunity to be selective about the projects on which we work, Desert Star didn't just appear fully formed as a brand known for quality, integrity, and excellence. I vividly remember our humble beginnings when it was just my father and me, and our total assets were a skill saw and a one-hundred-foot extension cord, worth $200. At one point, we took every job we could get, no matter the size, and I once went 26 months without taking a salary.

Desert Star has come a long way over the last forty-three years, and we've learned how to grow a business as well as how to build successful, healthy teams. We have seen the mountaintops, but we've also had our share of moments in the valley. While we are proud of our accomplishments, I don't think any of them would have been possible without learning many lessons the hard way.

One of the most important lessons I've learned is that we are better together. If anyone wants to build something great, they better have or develop a great team to help them.

Desert Star Construction currently has twenty-five team members, and those on our leadership team have an average tenure of twenty-three years. We also operate under the branding of Team DSC, which includes our team of twenty-five as well as the approximately 100 architects, de-signers, structural and mechanical engineers, lighting de-signers, and landscape architects and the roughly 800 trade contractors and suppliers with whom we work.

We absolutely would not be as successful as we are with-out the unique contribution of each and every one of our team members.

I trust you value your time as much as I do mine, so I hope you'll find the stories in this book useful. Through them, I hope to share some important principles that God has taught me as well as those hard-learned lessons earned over a life of building and leading teams and growing a suc-cessful construction business from the ground up. These principles will hopefully save you years of recovery from fail-ures. I am excited to share with you what's worked on my journey, and I pray it will help you on yours.

Introduction

I grew up in a culture where we were raised to know that Jesus is alive and still speaks to us today. I've experienced hearing His voice many times in the past, but I've also walked through seasons where I've allowed the stresses of life and leading a business to drown out His voice.

While I believe God is always speaking to us, in February of 2014 it had been many years since I could say with confidence that I had heard His voice or sensed His specific leading. Around that time, a youth pastor and his wife from our church invited my wife, Carol, and me to a leadership event in Scottsdale, Arizona for the volunteers at our church.

The event hosted some incredible speakers and opened with a time of praise and worship. Halfway through one of the worship songs, I felt something that I'd not sensed for many years, and I immediately knew it was God's presence. Standing there, tears welled up in my eyes, and I began to weep uncontrollably. God spoke to me that it was a time for simplification in every area of my life. While He didn't reveal His entire plan, God told me that this would be a time of preparation in my life: physically, emotionally, spiritually, and financially. He was preparing me for an upcoming season, not to just be productive locally. He was preparing me for something on a much larger scale.

Then I clearly saw an image of water rushing over the top of a reservoir's dam, and I audibly heard from God that He was going to pour out a blessing and open the floodgates. Malachi 3:10 immediately came to mind:

> Bring your full tithe to the Temple treasury so there will be ample provisions in my Temple. Test me in this and see if I don't open up heaven itself to you and pour out blessings beyond your wildest dreams. (MSG)

Carol and I have always believed that Jesus came to give rather than receive and that generosity is the hallmark of faith. While financial giving is an important aspect of tithing, we are also firm believers that God asks us to give the best of the gifts He's given us, whether that's our time, our talent, or our treasures. We are constantly seeking opportunities to share the knowledge, skills, and wisdom God has gifted us.

In response to my revelation from God, Carol and I immediately began to simplify all areas of our life. As we did,

God began opening doors of opportunity for us and providing new relationships and fresh perspectives. We were thrilled that God was rekindling our passions and giftings with His purpose and direction for the next chapter in our journey.

In 2014, Carol and I were blessed with the opportunity to spend time with Pastor Jentezen Franklin and his wife, Cherise. We became fast friends, and he's since had an immeasurable impact on our lives. I once asked him what's made the most impact on his life and ministry. He said, without a doubt, it was trust in God and fasting.

That was all we needed to hear. In 2015, Carol and I began our year with 21 Days of Prayer and Fasting in January as a way to seek God's will in every area of our life together for the year.

Fast forward to the end of 2019. It'd been several years since I'd heard from God about our season of preparation, and ahead of the 2020 fast, I felt spiritually dry. I was going through the motions of reading my Bible and praying, but I did not sense the enlightenment and revelation I was expecting. My daily readings had become more about what head knowledge I could gain, and my heart had become disconnected. I missed the quiet time of slowing down to listen for God's voice.

Desperate to have my faith reignited, I asked God to show me something that was unmistakably from Him. Part of my commitment in seeking God during the fast was to read through the New Testament to refocus on the consistency of His Word versus the shifting priorities of the world.

Unfortunately, I continued to struggle with distraction and was unfocused in prayer those first few weeks of 2020. The previous year had been filled with distractions, including months of emergency room visits, four surgeries, and three months of recovery for a gangrenous gallbladder and sepsis. Q4 looked nothing like I'd imagined. Though we'd had a record year in business, I was physically and emotionally bankrupt.

But I was desperate to hear from God, so I leaned in and kept at it. I'd come to a point in my life where I'd achieved so much personally and professionally that I wanted to spend the rest of my days giving away all that I've learned.

It had been over six years since I'd audibly heard from God, and I was anxious to move out of our season of preparation and start what was next—but I still didn't know what that looked like. I begged God to show me how He wanted to use all that He's done in and through me to help make a difference in the lives of others.

Then it happened. Like most mornings, I started by the firepit in our backyard, cup of coffee in hand, watching the sun light the early morning Arizona sky on fire.

I felt like most of my life was in order, that everything was going fine. But I still had that nagging feeling that something was missing. I felt my prayers were either unheard or unanswered, like they'd reach the ceiling and come bouncing back immediately.

At the time, I was reading about the Sermon on the Mount in Luke's Gospel. All I could think about was mountains, when God, as He so often does, opened my eyes in an instant of revelation. I'd been so focused on the mountain that I'd never considered what it meant when Jesus brought his apostles down to the "level place," publicly announced them, and then shared the Beatitudes with them and the multitudes.

I immediately knew this was the word from God I'd been waiting for. In one moment, He gave me a fresh perspective about how Jesus chose, appointed, and empowered his apostles (His leadership team) to expand His ministry and accomplish His will on earth.

Suddenly, all of our leadership successes and failures were colored with a new light. I saw clearly how our past wins aligned with Jesus' example and how our missteps came when we strayed from it.

Of course my prayers were being heard, and God was responding. Just not according to my timeline or in line with my expectations.

"It's leadership, Jerry," I felt God speaking to my heart. "From the moment I created you, I have given you opportunity after opportunity to lead: your school friends, your family, your peers, through your work, and in the marketplace. I've created you for such a moment as this—help others learn to lead like Jesus."

Still in Luke's Gospel, God took me from the Sermon on the Mount to the Sermon on the Plain, which I'll reference as the Sermon on the Level for the purposes of this book. It was there that God reminded me that even Jesus needed a trusted team of leaders to help Him accomplish His earthly mission to expand His ministry. It'd been six years, but God had finally brought me out of my season of preparation and set my mission in front of me. I knew this simple truth, and I needed to share it with other leaders: we simply cannot be successful alone.

Leading on the level is thinking about leadership from this perspective, about what we can learn from Jesus calling, appointing, and publicly affirming and empowering His apostles. Looking through this new lens, we can learn to lead like Jesus and turn our efforts from simple addition to seeing the fruits of our labor multiplied.

At times in my journey, I've felt stuck, inadequate, and unable to attract great people to join me in my vision for growing Desert Star Construction. What God revealed to me about leadership has changed my perspective completely. My hope is that you'll read this book with an open mind and an open heart so you, too, can experience the incredible impact that building healthy teams can make in your world.

If Jesus used these tools and changed the world, won't you use them to change yours?

1

On the Level

The construction guy (and geek) in me couldn't write a book titled *Leadership on the Level* without also talking a little more in-depth about levels.

I must admit that big box stores like Lowe's and Home Depot are like a candy store to me. I walk in, and I can't wait to see what's new. Unfortunately, for many decades, I would say that construction was at the hind end of technology. But this has changed, and I've also learned that just because a tool is new to me does not mean it's new to the industry.

Levels have been used for thousands of years, and they serve as such a unique image when thinking about leadership. Even the origination of the word, meaning "weight" or "balance," implies the importance of leading from a level place.

Approximately twenty years ago, I was watching a pool contractor set forms with a water level on one of our large resort pools. I'd never seen this before. It seemed primitive to me (we always used a laser level for these activities), and it started me down the path of researching the history of levels.

The first levels were primitive and used as early as 1100 B.C. when building the pyramids. They used boards with holes that were filled with water. When setting the board on the surface in question, they were easily able to determine if it was level by whether water stayed in the holes or overflowed.

About 1,000 years later, the Roman architect Vitruvius introduced a significantly larger instrument called the plank level. He used a plank approximately twenty feet in length with a groove in the top. The invention had perpendicular lines in it to determine if items were plumb along the vertical axis. This level was large and therefore not portable and seldom used.

Hero of Alexandria created a water level using two glass cylinders connected by a tube, born out of the belief that a body of water is always horizontal.

In 1630, the hose level was invented (a leather hose with a glass cylinder in each end) and was valuable when trying to level something that had no clear line of sight from one end to the other. There was a popular resurgence in this level in 1849 after vulcanized rubber became available, allowing the hose to remain flexible when wet for long periods of time.

When I was an apprentice carpenter, one of the journeymen asked me to get his whiskey stick. I had no idea what he was talking about (and I thought it was a bit early in the day to be drinking), but he was referencing his spirit level, an earlier version of what we now use. At the time, alcohol or other spirits were added inside the glass to prevent freezing. The sealed glass tube was originally straight, but it was improved to include a slight bend, lessening the erratic movement of the bubble.

My personal favorite came in 1989 in digital form. The bubble would tell you if the surface was level or plumb, but the digital level told you by how much. If a floor is a quarter inch out of level over the distance of 150 feet, it would be more than nine inches off from end to end! This can't help but make me see the importance of making sure our team building processes are healthy to ensure our team has a level place on which to pursue our shared vision and goals.

So, why the history lesson on levels? How does the level apply to our leadership?

1. We must realize that just because something is new to us, it does not mean it is new to our situation.

2. In leadership, you will always carry a weight, and it must be balanced.

3. When your tools are too burdensome, like the plank level, they will rarely be used.

4. Like the sealed tube, we must always be willing to bend a little in our methods (not our standards) to get a clear read on issues.

5. When you lead on the level, you are reaching your team's dreams and desires.

6. We should always seek the vertical (plumb) alignment to align with what God wants for us.

2

A Bit of
(Head-Scratching) History

As mentioned, I've spent over forty years building Desert Star Construction. I've seen the ups of booming economies and the bottoms fall out of housing markets.

While I'm a firm believer that God uses everything, the good and the bad, to teach us and grow our character, if there was any piece of advice I would have given to young Jerry, it would be to read the Bible and learn directly from Jesus the value of having a strong support team.

In the fall of 1979, our early organization, G. Meek Carpentry, performed rough and finish carpentry for commercial buildings as well as custom residential homes. My father and I ran the business and were fortunate enough to meet a leading architect in the Phoenix area who contracted us to work on four large custom homes for his firm. But he saw greater potential in us and suggested that we think seriously about taking steps to become general contractors.

At first, my father balked at the idea (he'd been burned in the past by an unethical business partner and was hesitant to re-enter the ownership side of a business). But we were tired of working for others and had grown weary of our paychecks consistently bouncing. We also knew the business, so after many discussions and weighing the pros and cons, we both agreed that it made sense as our next step.

My dad was an expert in construction, so we agreed that I would take on the management of the company, handling all the paperwork and administrative duties, finding and estimating work, executing contracts, managing human resources and payroll, and securing federal, local, and state permits (in addition to working fulltime on jobsites).

I'm not going to lie; it was a lot.

How did I find myself, a nineteen-year-old, responsible for running an entire contracting business that we'd begun with almost zero assets? It wasn't just my livelihood on the line; my father's and mother's were dependent upon our success, too.

During the first nine years of our company, everything seemed to happen in slow motion. All of our projects took longer and were more difficult than originally planned, and many ended up costing more than calculated.

I felt like I was in Neverland. There was never enough time for all the existing work we had under contract. Never enough time to find new business or enough money to hire new employees. Never enough capacity to pursue continued education and develop ourselves or our employees.

Part of my struggle was making up the deficit by working more hours. One responsibility after another was added to my plate as I carried the burden of not wanting to let my dad or my family down.

There are 168 hours in a week, and I tried to use each waking one of them working. My typical day began when I'd leave the house at 3:30 am and head for work, arriving early to prepare the jobsite for our crew with a generator, cords, and compressors. Our small crew would arrive and work from 5:00 am to 1:00 pm, and then we'd pack up everything, clean up the jobsite, and head home for the day.

But my day was just beginning. I'd head home for a quick shower and to take care of paperwork before driving back to the jobsite to complete the layout and saw work and make task lists for the following day.

In those days, I was physically strong and felt unstoppable, lifting large compressors and generators in and out of my truck without a second thought. But one day, while I was working alone, my back went out. I ended up laid out flat for nearly eighteen months.

This was the wake-up call I needed. I was no longer able to do everything myself and was forced to trust that those on our team would get the job done well. (At the time, this was a big ask, as I was high strung and stressed out most of the time!) Fortunately, my wife was handling all of the administrative responsibilities at this point, and my father stepped in to carry the responsibility of organizing the workload and the crew.

God had placed a vision on my heart to create and grow this company with my father. I didn't know exactly what or how to go about getting the help I needed at first, but this eighteen-month period confirmed that I wasn't going to get anywhere by myself.

(On a side note: While I was laid out on the floor, I had the joy of experiencing our eldest son's first steps. If I'd never been injured, I would almost certainly have been at work and missed what was such a special moment. I have no doubt God was working in more ways than one to teach me the value of slowing down and trusting others.)

So far, I'd been living by simple addition. The more work I put in, the more I thought I could grow our business. But if I was going to achieve my dreams of making the biggest impact on the most people by using my God-given gifts and talents, I would need help from a like-minded team to see the fruits of our labor multiplied.

As a builder, I know the value of creating a masterplan, and I can't help but smile and feel a bit of kinship with Jesus because He, too, was trained as a carpenter and knew the value of planning.

God had a masterplan to use Jesus to build and expand His Kingdom on earth, and Jesus recognized that He'd need a team of leaders to help Him achieve God's vision.

As we'll learn through the Sermon on the Level in the following chapters, Jesus was deliberate in choosing His team of leaders and publicly backing them as He sought to develop their leadership and expand His ministry.

As you work through the rest of this book, I invite you to learn from the Master Builder's example on how you can grow and develop a successful team as you pursue God's vision for your life.

Takeaways

1. Regardless of your current circumstances, stand firm in God's promise(s) to you.

2. To achieve your vision and mission, plan and prepare to lead a team of like-minded individuals.

3. Don't just add, multiply! Develop a strong team to enhance your efforts.

4. God had a masterplan and Jesus acknowledged His team in public.

Reflections

1. What vision has God placed on your heart?

2. In what areas are you currently working by simple addition, trying to achieve more by putting in extra time and energy yourself when you could be trusting others around you?

3. Why do you tend to rely more on yourself than seek the help of those around you?

3

Climbing the Mountain

One of those days Jesus went out to a mountainside to pray, and spent the night praying to God.

—Luke 6:12

If you've read this far, I trust you've realized the importance of having a strong team to help you achieve your goals. While I certainly learned this lesson the hard way, Jesus never took this simple truth for granted as He sought to accomplish the mission God gave Him of expanding His ministry on earth.

So, what's next? How do you select the right people? Where do you even begin?

Let's begin where Jesus did in the Sermon on the Level. At this point, Jesus had just been in a Galilean synagogue on the Sabbath, healing those in need. It was no doubt a contentious time, as the Pharisees sought to condemn Him for working on the Sabbath (among any other charge they could throw at Him).

Though He was now safely outside the synagogue and surrounded by so many of His followers, His first response was to climb a mountain alone and pray.

Jesus did not simply toss up a quick prayer as a formality; He prayed the whole night. In fact, the phrase "spent the whole night" originates from a rare Greek word used only once in the New Testament. This was a term used by physicians, like Luke, to describe an all-night vigil in the care of a patient.

It's encouraging to me that even Jesus, the Son of God, sought to find strength, wisdom, and fresh perspective in the presence of God before taking steps in the natural. As we see throughout His life, prayer was Jesus' first response rather than a last resort.

So, before choosing His main leadership team to help spread the Gospel—likely one of the most important and impactful decisions of His ministry—Jesus spent the entire night in prayer.

I often wonder the difference it would have made in my own life and career if I'd shared Jesus' conviction and dedication to prayer before making even the seemingly small decisions.

Too often, when I found myself in tenuous situations with any level of conflict, I automatically began thinking about potential solutions. My first response wasn't a response, it was a reaction, and it was one from my own strength. Unfortunately, it took me far too long to understand what we can undoubtedly learn from Jesus throughout the Bible, including the Sermon on the Level: prayerfully seeking God's will should also be our first response in everything we do.

While I have made it a point to pray over big projects throughout my career, I have also made hiring decisions that were seemingly no-brainers without first seeking God in prayer. As you can probably guess, these hires often resulted in stress, struggles, and strained relationships.

Building the right team has proven to be one of the most impactful things I've learned to do at Desert Star, and it can be the same for you. Just remember, when things go well, you're a hero, but when they don't, you're the goat. While hiring mistakes will happen, we shouldn't underestimate the impact they have on our existing team.

During a season of poor health, I needed a construction superintendent to help set the course and manage projects for our company. After reviewing over 100 applications, we made a hire and set a start date. To my surprise, I found out after the hire that, among many other red flags, our new superintendent did not have access to reliable transportation. Needless to say, it was not a good fit, and the relationship did not last long. What looked good on paper didn't translate to the culture of our company.

As a result, we learned from our mistake and now have a more thorough background check process as well as a more refined interview and vetting process.

But I also learned the valuable lesson that, as a leader, I'm always being observed. Making poor hires can compromise the confidence my team has in my ability to help them grow. The success of our company depends on bringing the right people onto our team, not just filling a position to check a box for our human resources team.

On the flip side, 2004 was a banner year for strengthening our team. Doug was working as a finish carpenter with a trade contractor for five years previously and was working on one of our country club projects at the time. Everything he did was excellent, and he was an incredible human being. My dad, who was superintendent, asked if I'd ever thought of adding him to the team. I hoped it would be a great fit (we needed a carpenter on staff, and we already knew Doug and his work).

What I didn't foresee at the time was that Doug would develop into a great superintendent. I trusted him, and he ended up serving as superintendent on every major remodel for homes built by Desert Star where I was the original superintendent. Doug is now a cornerstone of our concierge business and part of a team that provides proactive care and maintenance to Personal Resorts˚.

Doug's addition worked because we were prayerfully intentional about who we sought to add to our team and were committed to each other's success. When Doug joined the team, I told him not to worry about making mistakes—they happen, and we shouldn't waste our efforts or thoughts on them. (Although we should always learn from them so we don't repeat the same mistake.) I also told him that I had his back and that I trusted him.

There are many more stories of success where we prayed and sought God's perspective during the hiring process, but my point is this: who we choose to align ourselves with in leadership is a big decision and shouldn't be taken lightly. I now pray daily that God will surprise me in fresh and exciting ways with what He has for me and that He'll put the right people on my path. Now when we add to our team, I do so with both excitement and a weight of responsibility to help new team members grow and succeed.

As Jesus was faced with the task of beginning His public ministry, I can't help but think He climbed the mountain to obtain a different view of the decision in front of Him, both literally and spiritually.

As Jesus sought God's will in prayer, I think He received even more than He asked for. In my opinion, this is the moment when God asked Him to select His specific leadership team and elevate them from disciples (followers) to apostles (teachers).

This was a strategic step to move from simple addition by His own hand to the multiplication of His ministry that would continue long after He left earth. This is the moment that would influence the impact His ministry would have on this world.

Just as God was interested in Jesus' daily life and decisions, He is also concerned with ours, no matter how big or seemingly insignificant they may appear to us.

As leaders, are we making decisions out of our own strength on an empty tank? Or are we seeking God first in prayer, gaining His perspective, and making decisions that best align with His purpose for our lives? Regardless of your current answer to these questions, God is patiently waiting for you to meet with Him on the mountain.

Speaking of prayer, I'll never forget a message given by my youth pastor, who was a close friend and mentor as well. During a service one evening, he spoke from the Book of Joshua, referencing the moment when the leadership baton was passed from a recently deceased Moses to Joshua.

> Moses my servant is dead. Now then, you and all these people, get ready to cross the Jordan River into the land I am about to give to them—to the Israelites. I will give you every place where you set your foot, as I promised Moses. (Joshua 1:2-3)

I love the imagery in this passage of Scripture. In it, God promises to give Joshua every place upon which he walks, just as He'd promised Moses. What incredible confidence and authority this must have given Joshua. (But he only received it because He was submitted to God's will!)

I have bigger than average feet (size fourteen), which is probably one reason I took this message to heart from a young age. To this day, if I am walking, I believe that God is going to bless me wherever I go. This benefitted me as I started applying it to my business as well. I still walk the property line of every project, praying for God's will and asking Him to give me the places where the soles of my feet tread.

Why do I mention this here? It has helped me keep my focus on the right priority. I knew if we were awarded a contract, God was going to get us through it. If we were not successful in getting the project, I trusted God had a good reason why and never looked back.

This level of confidence and trust has taken so much stress out of my life. Just as Jesus prayed at the scene of the mountain, we should also pray first, seek God's will, and pray over the ground on which we hope to cover, trusting that He will align our steps and put the right people in our life. I hope that through prayer, you'll also begin to trust God in every area and to walk in the confidence of your God-given authority wherever He leads you.

Takeaways

1. Pray before even the smallest business decisions.

2. Poor hires can weaken your team's confidence in your leadership.

3. Continually look for the potential of current team members and elevate them to the appropriate next level.

4. Be certain that the ground you want to take is what God wants.

Reflections

1. How do you currently make decisions? Do you seek God in prayer first, regardless of the decision in front of you?

2. Where do you spend your focus? What is your priority, and is it the right one to help you achieve the vision God gave you?

3. Who do you know or are you currently working with that might be a great addition to your team?

4

Calling Your Team

When morning came, he called his disciples to him and chose twelve of them, whom he also designated apostles...

—Luke 6:13

I like to think of the gathering of the multitudes for the Sermon on the Level as possibly the first Mega-Church, and it's at this point, after hearing from God during a night of prayer, that Jesus calls the twelve to Him.

But how did He know who to choose? It was no small task considering the multitude surrounding Him. My belief is that, by His spirit, God pointed Him to those with whom He was already in close relationship. They loved being with

Him and being a part of His life. They were drawn to Him and committed to the relationship.

The Bible is filled with examples of God's Word pointing to the dangers of isolation and benefits of community. It's no surprise that Jesus recognized the importance of doing life together, of being in relationship with those around you, and knowing on whom you could depend.

In Luke's Gospel, it does not mention Jesus coming down to retrieve the twelve, and I believe He methodically called each one to climb the mountain one after the other. Their importance was being communicated by their calling, and I believe it helped to encourage them and fill them with a sense of purpose.

But before they could receive all that Jesus had for them, they had to be willing to climb the mountain, and I don't think any of them would have done so if they weren't aware of and committed to Jesus' vision.

I remember one summer when Desert Star was working on a loyal client's home—our third project on the same property. We were well under way, and I was surprised by how long the project was taking and how high the labor costs were. Something was off. I have learned to trust my instincts and drop in unexpectedly to see what's happening on projects.

A mentor of mine always reminded me that you get what you inspect, not what you expect. This became a part of my DNA as a leader, and I would visit project sites to check in or attend meetings as needed. After a few weeks inspecting this particular project, I noticed a trend with our carpenter and the site superintendent. It never failed; one or the other would always be outside the project, away from where most of the work was going on.

Come to find out, these two were acting as lookouts for each other, one warning the other when I was around so they could get back to work. Unfortunately, other contract workers were following this poor example and also taking advantage of the surveillance. This was a massive waste of our, and more importantly, our client's time and money, and it flew in the face of our company values.

These team members weren't ready to put in an honest day's work, much less climb the mountain and buy into the long-term vision of our team. On top of that, their poor behavior was negatively influencing other team members to follow their lead. So, we reevaluated and helped them find their future elsewhere.

Jesus understood it, and I can't stress enough the importance of establishing a clear vision for your company and your leaders and building your team accordingly.

In his book *Pearls of the King,* my friend Lee
Domingue speaks candidly about the dangers of what he
calls a "hireling spirit":

> This kind of an individual gives of his love and
> services with strings attached. He expects to be
> repaid for favors, he keeps track of offenses, and
> he will eventually think you owe him something
> for his "friendship." He will try to manipulate
> you to believe he is entitled to compensation of
> some sort and to make you feel guilty if you do
> not meet his requests. This kind of relationship
> cannot have any place. People like this are dis-
> tractions, never satisfied and will take you
> down.

Once the disciples had answered Jesus' invitation and
ascended the mountain, they were elevated to the position
of apostles. They were no longer one of the multitudes, but
a part of Jesus' inner circle who undoubtedly saw His ministry from a new perspective. They were His leadership team,
fully bought into His mission and appointed to lead in the
authority of Jesus' name.

Jesus prayed, sought God's will, and then chose from
those God had brought into His life who'd proven they were
bought into His mission.

Are we learning from Jesus' example and spending the same amount of care when choosing our leaders or filling empty positions on our team? Or are we more concerned with checking a box, filling a seat, and moving on?

Are we looking at those we know and who share our values, respect our mission, and will climb the mountain with us? Are our leaders willing to go the distance, or are they looking for a shortcut or the next best thing, regardless of where it comes from? Are they looking for a paycheck or a future with us?

Managing a business and leading a team is difficult enough in the best of circumstances. We shouldn't add to the stress by undervaluing the importance of selecting a strong support team.

I can tell you from experience that it's a much smoother journey to put the effort in on the front end—to ensure you're elevating the right people—than trying to heal organizational wounds resulting from a lack of leadership.

Takeaways

1. Be clear with your vision and mission—it will help you find the right individuals to partner with.

2. To ensure the company's integrity and values remain intact, always keep a finger on the pulse on your teams in some way. What gets measured gets done and can be improved upon.

3. Carefully evaluate potential new additions to the team to ensure they are a good fit for your vision as well as the team.

Reflections

1. What is your current process for adding members to your leadership team?

2. Have you ever had someone on your team with a hireling spirit? What was your experience, and what would you have done differently?

3. How can you go about elevating the *right* people from the start next time?

5

The Anatomy of a Team

> When morning came, he called his disciples to
> him and chose twelve of them, whom he also
> designated apostles: Simon (whom he named
> Peter), his brother Andrew, James, John, Philip,
> Bartholomew, Matthew, Thomas, James son of
> Alphaeus, Simon who was called the Zealot, Ju-
> das son of James, and Judas Iscariot, who be-
> came a traitor.
>
> —Luke 6:13-16

So far, we've seen Jesus climb a mountain and
pray to gain fresh perspective from God. We've also seen
Him call the twelve to Him on the mountain. But who were

these men, and can we learn anything about Jesus' decision to bring them into His inner circle?

As with everything Jesus did, His choice in apostles was intentional. These weren't random picks from the multitude, but selections from disciples with whom Jesus was in relationship and had done ministry and life with before this moment.

Their ranks included fishermen, a tax collector, a religious elite, a political zealot, and most likely tradesmen of some sort. A motley crew, indeed. I don't doubt that these twelve were wondering if Jesus had made the right choice. His selections almost certainly flew in the face of worldly wisdom, which would have pointed Him to the cultural, political, and religious leaders of the time.

But Jesus chose these men for a reason, and I believe He understood the value they brought to the team with their diversity of backgrounds, talents, and views. Not only that, but I like to imagine Jesus took a certain satisfaction in confounding expectations and using these men to help complete the most important work of His life. (See 1 Corinthians 1:27.)

Of course, Jesus knew that fishermen, accustomed to long, physically demanding hours would bring a strong work ethic, tenacity, and perseverance that would benefit His team as He called them to be fishers of men. Though Matthew (called Levi in Luke) was a tax collector for the government, I wonder if he or the other apostles had any idea that they'd learn that true wealth is found in relationship with Jesus. At the time, Jews anticipated a literal king to rise up and help them to overthrow Roman rule. How much greater was Simon's zeal when focused on helping to establish God's Kingdom that would ensure eternal freedom?

This rag-tag group of apostles learned at the feet of Jesus how to use their gifts, talents, and unique experiences to make a powerful impact on the world.

I'm willing to bet that each of us has team members with leadership potential right in front of us. But if we are unwilling to be intentional about praying over our decisions, seeking God's will, developing relationships, and connecting over shared goals and values, we may never have the eyes to see them.

Or just as scary, we run the risk of elevating the wrong people and seeing our teams and organizations struggle under the weight of unmet expectations and unclear leadership.

I previously mentioned hiring Doug, initially as a carpenter, but who is now an invaluable member of our leadership team. We also hired two others that same year, a welder/carpenter and a Construction Management graduate from Arizona State University who was working in roadbuilding and underground utilities. At first glance, these were hardly the heavy hitters with spotless resumes I would have looked for early on in my time leading Desert Star.

But God had opened my eyes to help me see the potential in those around me, to value their gifts and talents, and see them as He sees them.

I'm thrilled to share that with these three on our leadership team, we've learned to see problems from fresh perspectives, challenged each other to mature as leaders, and established a culture that values honest feedback, teamwork, and a desire to create unmatched quality and value for our clients.

As we've added diversely talented members to our team who are bought into our vision, we've seen unprecedented growth in the health of our team and the value of our business. In fact, from 2017-2020, we saw our revenue grow fourfold—talk about moving from simple addition to multiplication!

Do you know a carpenter with leadership potential? A welder just waiting for more responsibility? Perhaps you have your own road builder on your team right now. You'll never find them if you don't ask God to help you seek them out.

In our journey, we've also looked for different ways to approach personal development and hiring, often looking beyond the typical construction avenues. For customer care, we've studied everyone from Ritz Carlton to the Mayo Clinic, and it's made a huge impact on how we think about problem solving and improvement.

We also apply this approach to our hiring process. For executive assistants and project coordinators, we look at mortgage brokers and banking customer service associates as well as within other segments of the construction community, including commercial contractors and production homebuilders.

Jesus saw through the world's expectations and made deliberate decisions about whom to elevate to His team. Just as He knew then, we have learned that spotless resumes are a dime a dozen and are no guarantee of success. We've learned the value in hiring those with integrity and the character to work through tough situations, learning from diverse viewpoints, and teaching the skills we need to be successful.

Takeaways

1. Develop a unified team that has diverse backgrounds, talents, and viewpoints.

2. Pray over hiring decisions prior to adding team members.

3. Diversify your problem-solving process.

4. Look at your team to see if they have undeveloped talent.

Reflections

1. What is your current process for adding to your leadership team? Do you look for a certain "type" to fill every position?

2. How do you think different viewpoints and experiences would add value to your team?

3. How do you resource your team? What value could be added by learning from leaders outside your industry?

6

Empowering Your Team

When they came down from the mountain, the
disciples stood with Jesus on a large, level area,
surrounded by many of his followers and by the
crowds. There were people from all over Judea
and from Jerusalem and from as far north as the
seacoasts of Tyre and Sidon.

—Luke 6:17 NLT

As Jesus brought His newly-appointed apostles
down the mountain, I can only imagine what it was like to
be a member of the gathering crowds. They'd likely been up
all night, anticipating the presence of Jesus and hoping to
hear from Him and be healed of various sicknesses. Then,

for the first time since ascending to pray and choose His team of apostles, Jesus appeared, confidently leading twelve men down the side of the mountain as the sun rose behind them.

While I like to think that Jesus called each apostle up the mountain individually, I believe He brought them down together, unified as a team. It is also worth noticing that Jesus didn't come down the mountain, stop at an elevated position, and then begin teaching. He also didn't immediately join the crowds and heal the sick in His presence. Instead, He stopped on a level place with the apostles, turned to them, and gave them the first of the Beatitudes.

This is a powerful visual image and is the first time the multitudes have seen who Jesus empowered. At this point, the apostles were no longer part of the audience but were in front of everyone, just behind Jesus, on equal ground.

I believe this was an intentional step taken by Jesus to publicly affirm the apostles as members of His leadership team, bestowing on them a new authority in the presence of the multitudes. I also think the Beatitudes spoke to important felt needs of the people gathered as well as to those they would encounter in the world.

But were the apostles ready the day Jesus selected them? How much did they really understand about what had just happened?

When Jesus made His selection, He was also clear on laying out expectations. He moved immediately from elevating them to laying out the discourse on discipleship, basically saying through the Beatitudes, "If you want to follow Me, this is what you can expect." Are we that precise when we lay out our expectations to our team?

Jesus commanded His followers to make disciples of all nations, proclaim the Kingdom of God, and heal the sick (Matthew 28:19, Luke 9:2), but not before He selected the twelve apostles and poured His own life into them for approximately three years. Whether they felt prepared or not, they were stepping into uncharted territory to begin hands-on training.

Talk about the ultimate job training program! These men were present as Jesus spoke parables and performed miracles—as he brought sight to the blind, raised the dead to life, and spoke truth to the spiritually bankrupt. I have no doubt that the experience the apostles gained at the feet of Jesus prepared them to fulfill the Great Commission after Jesus was no longer present to lead them.

Similarly, I've always found it easier to grow and internalize teachings when I am able to experience them firsthand. Jesus' example begs the question—are we pouring into our leaders? Are we teaching them all that we know, or are we holding back? Are we giving our best to our teams, equipping them to be successful without us?

Growing up, I had eight Italian uncles who worked in varying aspects of the construction industry, and watching them work gave me interesting perspectives. One day I asked one of my uncles why he did not tell my cousin how to complete a specific task. My uncle said that he always holds something back, whether it's information or a skillset, so his employees will need him (and probably not leave the company). In contrast, my dad taught me construction and insisted that I learn how to do every aspect of the job. He shared all he knew with the hope that I would surpass what he knew and had accomplished. I have committed to do the same for my sons and our team.

Empowering your team does not mean leaving them to fend for themselves after you've elevated them. Jesus didn't do this to His apostles, and we shouldn't do this to our teams either. If we are not investing in the right people and giving them our best, they'll never reach their full potential and our teams will suffer as a result.

For our team, empowerment is a gradual process that begins with building relationships and spending time with newly appointed leaders on job sites, ensuring they're not in over their head, answering their questions, asking their perspective about decisions they are making, and occasionally helping them adjust course.

We empower by design, not by default. In fact, in the early days, I gave too much authority to new leaders too soon and was not as involved in their growth as I should have been, and our leaders suffered in ambiguity.

It's important that we spend time teaching, but it's just as important to give some space for our leaders to make mistakes and learn from them—they need the authority to own aspects of a project if they're ever going to grow.

Spending time with new leaders to review each phase of a job is a big commitment, but investing this time has paid off with multiplication of what they achieve personally as well as how they contribute to the company's overall success—especially when we are no longer present to walk them through a job.

I mentioned in the previous chapter how we seek out talented members from outside the construction industry to add to our team. We also place a high value on formal and informal education as well as equipping and empowering our leaders to succeed. We are always looking for ways to engage, educate, and develop our team members.

We sponsor and attend leadership events, invite guests from outside the construction industry to learn from, read and discuss books together. We even provide tuition reim-bursement to our team and help fund multiple scholarships at Arizona State University for those who want to pursue a career in the trades.

Jesus knew that His apostles would one day be respon-sible for leading the Church without His physical presence, so He spent time training, educating, and empowering them to be successful after His departure. We, too, should follow this example and prepare our teams to lead and be successful when we aren't around to guide their every step.

Takeaways

1. Unify your team by showing them their individual and collective strengths.

2. Clearly communicate and set expectations.

3. Equip your team members in every way you can so they can achieve their full potential—when they win, you win and vice versa.

4. Give your best to your leaders.

5. Empower by design, not default. Spend quality time with each team member and learn their unique giftings and viewpoints.

6. Give your team members grace and space to grow and develop themselves.

Reflections

1. How do you empower your leaders? Have you ever acknowledged them publicly to walk in authority?

2. Do you teach your teams all you know so they can be successful? If not, how would their world look different if you did?

3. How do you promote unity within your organization and your leadership team(s)?

7

The Beautiful Attitudes

After descending the mountain with His apostles and joining them on level ground, Jesus' first action was to turn to His apostles and provide them four specific Beatitudes in full view of the gathering crowds. I believe He did this as a signal, to both His apostles and the multitude, that those with him on that level place were His inner circle, bestowing on them an authority to work on His behalf. At this point, the apostles were no longer mere students. They were messengers-in-training, co-owners of the responsibility of sharing the Gospel and growing the early Church.

As with anything Jesus does, there's usually more than meets the eye, and there's almost always a lesson that points toward eternity. Though Jesus provided plenty of additional teachings to the apostles and the multitudes at the Sermon on the Level, it's my belief that He was speaking first on what mattered most to the present crowd.

These first four Beatitudes (or beautiful attitudes as I like to call them) spoke primarily to pains, struggles, and difficulties that everyone faces at one point or another in their life. So, when Jesus said that true disciples, though poor, hungry, weeping, and rejected are blessed, I believe He was working to shift our perspective to the eternal. These first four Beatitudes were for the masses, while I think the remaining were to be developed by the apostles. Jesus met people, including the multitudes, at the place of their greatest need and spoke to them at the heart level. "Get these right, and help others to learn their importance," I imagine He said, "and you'll be blessed beyond your wildest imagination."

So, what did Jesus mean when He said we are "blessed" when poor, hungry, weeping, and rejected? As Charles Swindoll references in *Insights on Luke*, it describes a "transcendental joy, the kind that neither depends on earthly fortunes nor falters before temporary hardships. A blessed person possesses joy beyond their circumstances."

Can you imagine joy *in spite* of circumstance? Knowing that your success isn't entirely up to you? Having contentment no matter your accomplishments or the size of your bank account? Confidence in the face of an economic recession, hope regardless of a negative diagnosis, or peace in the midst of any storm?

We all walk through peaks and valleys in our personal and professional lives, and I believe the four beautiful attitudes Jesus spoke to during His Sermon on the Level are critical to understanding how we can shift our perspective from the worldly to the eternal and, in doing so, learn to thrive and find joy in every situation.

Takeaways

1. Determine what matters to your team members. They have your vision at heart, but what is their vision for themselves? Their vision to enhance your vision?

2. Empower your team by speaking to them at a heart level, as Jesus did. Don't speak at them; speak to them.

3. Create a workplace culture that encourages your team members to thrive rather than merely survive.

Reflections

1. Is this definition of "blessed" new to you? If so, how has your perception changed?

2. Think of a time when you or your team faced adversity and circumstances outside of your control—how did you respond?

3. Does your team survive or thrive? How can you help them move from a "got to" to a "get to" attitude towards pursuing your shared vision?

8

Blessed Are the Poor

Looking at his disciples, he said: "Blessed are you who are poor, for yours is the kingdom of God."

—Luke 6:20

In our society, we have so many choices: what to do, what to eat, which show to watch or book to read. If we're not careful, we can succumb to paralysis by analysis before we've laced up our shoes and left the house in the morning. So how do successful people ultimately decide what to focus on?

Just as Jesus did, successful people never lose sight of their mission. They keep it as the central focus of their work and then act on what will achieve the best results.

For Jesus, He saw the needs of the people.

Proverbs 10:22 says, "The blessing of the Lord brings wealth, and he adds no trouble." If that's true, then why did Jesus start out with the assertion that poverty is a blessed state? It would have grabbed my attention when He said it, as I'm certain it grabbed the attention of all those in attendance. And I have no doubt that it was a tough pill to swallow.

I've worked paycheck to occasionally bounced paycheck, and it's miserable. As I noted earlier, there was also a time in my life when I went twenty-six months without an income. My favorite bumper sticker at the time was "Why can't I pay my MasterCard with my Visa?" Being broke made me feel inadequate and gave me a sense of powerlessness, which I think is partly the point Jesus was making—let that realization point you to God.

In the Message translation, Jesus says, "You're blessed when you've lost it all. God's kingdom is there for the finding." (Luke 6:20) He is clearly speaking about those who realize their own helplessness and spiritual inadequacy. The word poor here actually means "to be destitute" or "bankrupt," and Jesus is referencing spiritual bankruptcy.

But what exactly is spiritual bankruptcy? According to D. A. Carson, we are poor in spirit when we know there is nothing within us, not family ties, community respect, occupation, good works, or personal "holiness" that can earn favor with God.

As an illustration, Carson says, "We are blessed when we understand that we are all just beggars coming to the door of God's Kingdom without anything to get us in. So, we pound on the door, appealing to the King, O Lord, let me in; O Lord, give me what is needed for entrance—your grace and mercy."

Ultimately, Jesus was taking the worldly perception that wealth provides comfort and security and turning it on its head, pointing to the reality that those who are "poor in spirit" are able, because of their realization and acceptance of their own insufficiency, to find true wealth and joy in Jesus.

When the economy tanked in 2008, the Phoenix construction market collapsed along with it. A large chunk of this fell on my head, as Desert Star lost $25 million in work over a forty-five-day period. Talk about coming to the end of your own ability!

I sat down with our team and shared my thoughts: "If we were to choose a business to be in at this moment, it would not be construction." Everyone was frozen in shock.

With that on the table, we presented a plan for how we would press on.

I told our team that we were not going to participate in the recession, and that neither I nor my wife Carol, who runs office operations, were going to take a paycheck until the economy turned around. (It took almost two years before our family's income resumed.) I also told them that nobody would be laid off.

I didn't know what to do, but I asked God often for the next steps. I remember reading through the book of Daniel and his prayer of "not for my sake, but for yours, Lord" (Daniel 9:19) striking a chord with me. I had no choice but to lean into God. So many people were aware of my faith, and I spent many early mornings and late nights crying out to God for strength, that He would show Himself faithful in this season for His sake.

Boy did He ever show up. Rather than hunker down, we felt called to do the opposite. We invested in our team and in our community, refocusing our business on high-end sustainable building.

We contacted previous clients and sent crews out to perform any deferred maintenance on their homes at no charge, just to keep our team busy. But our clients chose to pay us anyway, and referrals for new projects started coming in.

Our boldest response was to embrace a green building venture. In 2009, we added the first LEED AP (Leadership in Energy and Environmental Design Accredited Professional) for homes in Arizona to our team: our son, Jeremy.

We dove into the deep end with a multimillion-dollar LEED Gold commercial renovation that required thirty-two permits to be submitted and approved within a five-month period, start to finish, including design.

With this project's success, God helped me put two and two together. Sustainability was in our company's DNA, so we decided to take the sustainability movement and apply it to luxury homes, which has been a perfect fit for our mission and values.

I will never call the housing market downturn a good thing—two years of lost wages was rough. But in the midst of it, God allowed me to come to the end of myself, and He led me in a direction that I never would have gotten to on my own. Faced with the choice to either shrink our company or invest in it, between austerity and targeted stimulus, God humbled me and led me to choose the latter.

It took sacrifice, courage, and a lot of prayer and faith in God's plan, but we kept our team intact, expanded our capabilities, reconnected with our clients, and raised the company's profile in the community.

We shouldn't be surprised that Jesus' first Beatitude was about poverty. Jesus warned us that those who pursue wealth above all else have already received their reward in this life. God doesn't want or need our money—He desires our hearts. Is our trust in our paycheck and our balance sheet? The awards on our shelf? Or do we lean into Jesus and believe that He will meet our needs regardless of what we face personally or professionally?

While Jesus was busy shifting people's perspectives, it's also important to understand what He was not saying. Jesus didn't mean that obtaining wealth is inherently bad, but that choosing present-day gratification over eternally important things is dangerous and will only result in temporary satisfaction. In short, do the things of this world own us, or the other way around?

Another consideration is that perhaps the wealthy Jesus spoke of are those who gained their wealth at the expense of others. Whatever wealth someone has should not come through unethical compromise or the adoption of "everybody is doing it" business practices. Jesus was reminding His apostles and everyone listening about the dangers of the love of money and holding worldly possessions so tightly that they forget where true wealth is found. It was a reminder of the blessedness of spiritual poverty and of living open-handed. Jesus' words are always pointing us towards eternity—our true reward is found at the end of our race and will be a result of what we did with what God gave us.

My friend and mentor, Lee Domingue, has been resolute and consistent in encouraging me and others to live open-handed and leave a legacy rather than build a dynasty.

How heartbreaking would it be to live a life of extravagance only to find yourself in God's presence and learn that you completely missed the mark, that your life failed to make an eternal impact!

Takeaways

1. Determine your goals and actively work on defining your vision.

2. Know that no matter how smart, creative, talented, or successful you are, you always need to rely on the Lord for strength and life.

3. Engage in creative ways to work through tough business seasons and be committed to moving forward with your team.

Reflections

1. Is the idea of spiritual bankruptcy new to you? If so, how can this new perspective help you lead more effectively?

2. Have you had a moment where you've come to the end of your own ability? How did it make you feel, how did you respond, and what did you learn from it?

3. What do you hold onto too tightly in this world? How can you move from dynasty building to leaving a lasting legacy?

9

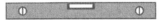

Blessed Are the Hungry

*Blessed are you who hunger now, for you will
be satisfied.*

—Luke 6:21a

When I first read this verse, my mind immediately strayed toward food, and it reminded me of when I was suddenly cast into the caretaker role for my wife, who suffered a devastating and rare type of heart attack. This event put all that my wife does into perspective, and one evening she asked me which of those activities was my least favorite. I had plenty to choose from: laundry, dishes, cooking, cleaning, driving her to appointments, finances, and grocery shopping.

Hands down, my least favorite was grocery shopping. Even with a list that Carol would help me make, I was clueless as to where anything in the grocery store was located. Carol has always helped us to eat healthy and clean because she would only buy foods that were good for us. However, I like to snack, and now I had free reign to buy whatever caught my eye (cereals, cookies, chocolate, or yogurt covered pretzels). I was like a kid at a candy store (or a Jerry at a grocery store!).

I started eating all the wrong foods. It was terribly unhealthy, and I was always left unsatisfied. While it definitely is true for food, it also helped me to understand the deeper spiritual truth that Jesus spoke to in this Beatitude: Unless I'm consuming the right things, I will never be satisfied.

I like reading the same verse in different translations to help my understanding. Notice what is said between the King James Version and The Message Bible.

> Blessed are ye that hunger now: for ye shall be filled. (Luke 6:21 KJV)

> You're blessed when you're ravenously hungry. Then you're ready for the Messianic meal. (Luke 6:21 MSG)

This meal is something only Jesus can provide and is called the Messianic meal. We should note that the Greek word for "blessed" is makários, which means "happy, jubilant.

Let's look at this verse with a new emphasis: "You're blessed (*happy and jubilant*) when you're ravenously hungry. Then you're ready for the Messianic meal." Luke 6:21 The Message (Emphasis mine).

This message is not for the stomach, but for the soul and spirit. Jesus didn't mean that those who starve themselves are blessed. He was talking about hunger at a spiritual level and the joy of delayed gratification found by those who forego feeding themselves only on the things of this world in favor of God's Word and His ways. Faith in Jesus offers an eternal solution—it is the only thing that will truly satisfy our hunger.

The word satisfied literally means, "fed or filled with enough." So, according to Jesus, those who hunger for righteousness, for His ways, will receive satisfaction in their souls beyond anything even the best of this world could offer.

Unfortunately, I've also learned this lesson the hard way. During the first two decades of our business, our tax bill was of little concern to me (the revenue and profits were so small as to be inconsequential). As our business grew, we saw great profits, and I became obsessed with finding a way to reduce our tax burden.

Out of the blue, I received a call from someone I'd known for years who had a real estate investment in Kansas City, Missouri that needed a financial backer. Based on the pro-forma, past history, and the photos, this was a sure thing. All I needed to do was provide a personal guarantee for $500,000.

Things went well at first, before they changed quickly. Unforeseen costs, cash calls, extended construction time-lines—it was an epic failure, and I was to blame.

In the middle of the night, one year after we'd started, I woke up soaked in sweat. As soon as Carol woke up, I asked her to check our personal bank accounts. The bank had swept funds from all of our accounts. What about the cash calls for the Kansas City project or the $500,000 that was immediately due and payable? It was all gone, never to be recovered.

My motives weren't submitted to God. I was simply hungry to reduce our financial burden, and even worse, I didn't pray or read God's Word before making the decision. We personally took a hit because of my misplaced priorities. It took us many years to pay off everything and break even, and it was a painful lesson learned.

I also love how one of Luke's fellow apostles, Matthew, talks about this same Beatitude:

> You're blessed when you've worked up a good appetite for God. He's food and drink in the best meal you'll ever eat. (Matthew 5:6 MSG)

Of course, we need food to sustain our life here on earth, but I encourage you to recognize the importance of finding your soul's source of fulfillment in Jesus. While the hunger pangs of this world are an important physical indicator, let them also lead you to God—He wants to share a meal with you, and He's the only source that will always leave you satisfied.

Takeaways

1. It is easy to give in to societal pressures when it comes to your business, but these are the times to lean in and trust the Lord.

2. Check your motives daily. Feeding on the things of this world will always leave you unsatisfied and hungry for more.

3. Change your perspective—delayed gratification is a gift.

4. Remain happy and jubilant regardless of the circumstances.

Reflections

1. What do you hunger for the most every day? How does it align with the vision God gave you?

2. Have you experienced trials as a result of hungering after something with the wrong motive(s)?

3. How can you feed your spiritual hunger for God? What benefits do you think this would provide in your life?

10

Blessed Are the Brokenhearted

Blessed are you who weep now, for you will laugh.

—Luke 6:21b

I have walked through many dark times, both personally and professionally, when all I wanted to do was curl into a ball and drown myself in tears of sorrow. When we saw great financial struggles early in our company history and I wasn't sure we were going to make it. Or when our daughter Hannah was born at twenty-eight weeks and died eight days later. Or when our youngest son Jonathan was born at twenty-four weeks and weighed just two pounds.

Carol and I were heartbroken, but her doctor gave us advice that has stuck with us for decades: surround yourself with people who love you unconditionally and won't judge you, regardless of how you feel in the moment. From that moment forward, we decided to make the pain and challenges we face steppingstones to our future rather than tombstones. We are also determined that our trials will be another chapter in our story, that we'll use what we've learned to walk alongside others experiencing difficult times.

I think the revelation we had points to the heart of what Jesus was getting at in this third Beatitude. Nowhere in the Bible does God promise Christians a pain-, struggle-, or stress-free life. In fact, He promises the opposite:

> I have told you these things, so that in me you may have peace. In this world you will have trouble. But take heart! I have overcome the world. (John 16:33)

We live in a fallen world, and there are sources of pain and heartache everywhere: lost people, poverty, famine, disease, abuse, division, family stresses—the list goes on.

But Jesus wasn't saying that pain and sorrow were a source of blessing. Rather, He was once again shifting our perspective to the eternal. While pain wasn't the blessing, a godly response to the pain we endure and the trials we face can draw us closer to God, provide us with a peace that surpasses understanding, and equip us to help others walking through their own trials. Quite simply, what breaks God's heart should also break ours.

In the Old Testament, God honored those who wept for righteousness. In Psalm 126:5-6, we see those tears as seeds that produce a harvest of goodness in the future. Any of us who weep over what is wrong in this world have a greater chance of being part of the solution.

In business, some leaders focus only on the client. Increased revenue is great, but how could we accomplish anything truly great on our own? At Desert Star, we've always strived to value everyone the same, from the client to the carpenter and everyone in between, with this word from Proverbs at the heart: *The rich and the poor shake hands as equals—God made them both!* (Proverbs 22:2 MSG)

We know that we are only as strong as our team, and when they hurt, we hurt right along with them. Toward the end of our second decade in business, a team member of ours who'd been with us nearly five years fell ill and was out longer than anticipated. This was long before we had the disability benefits that are currently in place, and we knew we had to do something once his sick time was used.

He had a wife and children, and it broke our hearts to think that he wouldn't be able to care for them. So, we made certain that he had funds equivalent to his wages so he could.

I hesitate to share this type of story because it can come across as self-congratulatory or be mistaken for pride. But I can't stress enough the importance of letting God soften you to the people around you and the things that break His heart. People are our most valuable commodity, and they trump profits every time.

Similarly, one of our trade contractor's employees was working on a large project when they fell off a scaffolding. We loved this man—he was a dedicated, focused, and kindhearted person who was taking great care of the project.

During his recuperation, we learned he was experiencing financial hardship. So, we found out where he lived and made a delivery of groceries and money. We didn't realize until years later how much of an impact this simple kindness made on him and his wife. A year later, he interviewed and joined our team and is now in his eleventh year with us. He later shared how important it was for him to join a team where people are valued and cared for—we never knew how the seeds we planted would grow!

As a leader in your organization, I don't think it's possible to appreciate and care for your people too much.

As we respond to the brokenness around us, let's also not forget the importance of joy, humor, and laughter. Yes, Jesus was serious about His Father's business, and His heart broke for those hurting around Him. But He was also joy-filled, celebratory, and someone who loved to share a good meal and conversation. He was someone who children flocked to and climbed all over!

Having an empathetic heart for the pain of others and walking in joy are not mutually exclusive. If we are to weep over what makes God weep, we should also celebrate what He celebrates and live joyful lives that points others to Him.

As King Solomon said in Ecclesiastes:

> There is a time for everything, and a season for
> every activity under the heavens...a time to
> weep and a time to laugh, a time to mourn and
> a time to dance. (Ecclesiastes 3:1,4)

Or as Solomon mentions again in Proverbs 17:22—a cheerful heart is good medicine.

The need for laughter in the church was also highlighted by missionary statesman Oswald Sanders:

> Should we not see that lines of laughter about
> the eyes are just as much marks of faith as are
> the lines of care and seriousness?

Just as important as caring for and walking alongside those experiencing difficulties is cultivating a culture of joy and family. We work hard, so we like to enjoy life and celebrate the victories, especially after overcoming struggles and navigating obstacles.

We've had many successful Family Fun weekends over the years, where the entire team and their families are invited to spend the weekend together in celebration. On one of the weekend trips, we rented an island for the day on a lazy river at the Westin. At our Friday night dinner, we handed out waterproof cameras, money for families to use, and bags of snacks for their rooms. During dinner, we had the hotel deliver monogrammed towels and blow-up toys for the children along with a pump (inflating those on your own is no fun!).

It's also been a joy to watch as our team has become more involved with the planning of these celebrations and has taken ownership over the culture of our company. Every event we spend together builds unity in our team as we grow our relationships.

Just as celebrating the wins is a valuable team-builder, a godly response when things go sideways will help build trust and resiliency within your team as well as foster hope for the future.

Jesus wants to replace our sorrow with a joy that will sustain us now and reward us in Heaven, and He calls us to be empathetic toward those around us. How we handle the brokenness of our world and the challenges we face daily makes a huge impact on those around us, including the teams we lead.

Takeaways

1. Use what you've learned through trials to empower others.

2. As difficult as they may be, trials can be a gateway to a closer relationship with the Lord.

3. People are the most valuable commodity, and they should trump profits every time.

4. Value all the people you work with – God sees them as the same.

5. The way that we manage our trials with integrity and honesty can have a great impact on our team.

Reflections

1. How do you and your leaders respond to the heartbreak and trials of those on your team?

2. Think about some of the greatest trials you've walked through. How can you use what you learned to pour into those around you when they're facing their own struggles?

3. How can you graciously love on your team or your clients who are in need, even when it doesn't make the most business sense?

11

Blessed Are the Rejected

*Blessed are you when people hate you, when
they exclude you and insult you and reject your
name as evil, because of the Son of Man.*

—Luke 6:22

Talk about a hard sell on the Beatitude of rejection—why would anyone want to embrace this? On the surface, it's all about the downside with no visible upside. I often think about the rejection that Jesus endured, and, if I'm honest, I'm glad I haven't had to experience anything close to it.

At this point in the scripture, the twelve apostles may have been embraced by Jesus, but they certainly weren't accepted by the dominant social and political bodies of the time. Jesus promised the apostles, and anyone who followed Him, that they would be on the wrong end of hatred, social rejection, and defamation of character, just for associating with Him!

For clarity we should know that this would have resonated within their Jewish culture, where a great fear was excommunication from the community. Though the worldly cost to follow Jesus was a steep price to pay (financial, social, cultural, etc.), the apostles recognized the eternal value in following Jesus. They feared being cut off from their relationship with God more than they feared being cut off from the world around them.

I think Jesus was well aware of how difficult life would be for His followers, as well as how standing firm in faith could impact the world for His Kingdom.

I'm a big Charles Spurgeon fan, and I find it humbling that even such a great champion of the faith struggled in the face of rejection. During a stressful time in his life, when Spurgeon was depressed by the criticism he faced, his wife took a sheet of paper, printed the Beatitudes on it, and tacked it to the ceiling over his bed. She knew it, and she wanted it to be a reminder to him when he woke and when he laid down at night: everyone who lives righteously will face persecution.

To be persecuted like Jesus talked about should be like wearing a badge of honor. Jesus encouraged those who endured persecution to "rejoice and be glad." Historically, the persecuted belonged to a noble group of Old Testament prophets who were ultimately rewarded in heaven.

True, that doesn't make it easy to face criticism and the harsh voices of rejection. But Jesus was again shifting our perspective to the eternal and the impact we can make on others by standing firm in our faith, our values, and our identity in Christ.

When our sons were growing up, we taught them how to avoid compromising situations by encouraging them to know their answer before the question was asked. Of course, the same principle applied to us, and we've had our own opportunities to stand firm.

In the early years of our business, I was working on my first project that was over a million dollars, and the client offered me $1.2 million in cash for a $1.4 million project. He said I could get ahead by not having to pay taxes.

I thanked him for the offer but immediately let him know that I couldn't accept, saying "If I were to take this money, how would you ever be able to trust me?" If I had taken the money, he would have had every right to doubt my integrity in every situation and transaction. Fortunately, we went on to build his home by the book, and he's become one of our most avid supporters (we've done several more projects together since).

Sad but true, Christians are often persecuted not for their Christianity but for their often-un-Christlike behavior. Everything I have studied and learned in the Bible speaks to the value of a strong work ethic, integrity, and excellence.

One story almost forty years ago comes to mind, when I was just 21 and working a job for a huge client (our first for the CEO of a publicly held company). We'd worked hard to come in on time and under budget for his home, but I was disappointed at what I heard during a dinner table debrief—everyone was left with a negative impression of our plumbing contractors, who happened to be Christians. It wasn't because of their faith, but instead, the focus was on their poor work ethic causing delays and quality issues.

The morning after the client's first night in the house, he called me to ask if the toilet was supposed to have hot water when he flushed. I could have died on the spot. I tried to play it cool and told him there was no charge for the steam. We shared a laugh, and I asked him not to use the toilet until the plumbers could re-pipe (hot water had the potential to crack the porcelain toilet).

Unfortunately, the plumbing contractor felt persecuted because of his faith when we held him accountable for the toilet as well as many other items.

Please notice that this Beatitude does not say, "Blessed are you when you don't fulfill your contract, when you are late, when you provide poor quality and service."

I understand, sometimes people have difficult personalities, or they can be rude, insensitive, or thoughtless—even piously obnoxious. The world also rejects those discerned as proud, judgmental, lazy, or irresponsible. Unfortunately, too many Christians can feel persecuted for all the wrong reasons, without taking a long hard look in the mirror.

Don't fall prey to the delusion that all rejection you face is because of Christ. Stand strong in your identity in Christ, but also understand that this identity calls us to a higher standard of excellence in all areas so that we can be a beacon of light to those around us.

I want to encourage you to be your best self and build a respectable reputation (not perfect), and to allow that reputation in this world to become your testimony. There is an old saying: "Even a dead dog can swim with the tide." To swim against the tide, you must be alive, fully alive! If you are persecuted for Christ, be thankful that He is fully alive within you. To make a difference, we need to swim against the current and stand firm in our values. If we don't, we're liable to be battered about by the whims of culture, and we'll never fully walk out the vision God has given us.

Takeaways

1. Embody your values consistently and be prepared for compromising situations that could make you waver or doubt them.

2. Standing firm in your values will garner respect from others.

3. Excellence is a biproduct of your identity in Christ.

Reflections

1. How have you faced rejection for standing firm in your faith and identity in Christ?

2. Have you ever dealt with Christians who play the perse-cution card to cover their own professional shortcomings? How did this make you feel, and what did you take away from the experience?

3. How can you start building a respectable reputation that will serve as your testimony to the world around you?

12

Salt and Light

You are the salt of the earth. But if the salt loses its saltiness, how can it be made salty again? You are the light of the world. A town built on a hill cannot be hidden...In the same way, let your light shine before others, that they may see your good deeds and glorify your Father in heaven.

—Matthew 5:13a,14,16

The year was 1972, and my family had just relocated from New York to Arizona—I was beginning my freshman year of high school in my eighth different school. It was during this season that I accepted Jesus Christ as my Savior and everything changed in a positive way for me.

I became close friends with my youth pastor, and he adamantly encouraged me to read the New Testament. When I reached chapter five in the Book of Matthew, I came across the Beatitudes given by Jesus on the Sermon on the Mount.

Many years later, as I previously mentioned, it dawned upon me that these are the beautiful attitudes that describe what our inner character should be as fully devoted followers of Jesus. These are many of the same Beatitudes found in Luke's Sermon on the Level, though Matthew's version immediately follows them with a statement from Jesus about being salt and light. I love how this scripture is translated in The Message Bible:

> Let me tell you why you are here. You're here to be salt-seasoning that brings out the God-flavors of this earth. If you lose your saltiness, how will people taste godliness? You've lost your usefulness and will end up in the garbage.
>
> Here's another way to put it: You're here to be light, bringing out the God-colors in the world. God is not a secret to be kept. We're going public with this, as public as a city on a hill. If I make you light-bearers, you don't think I'm going to hide you under a bucket, do you? I'm putting you on a light stand. Now that I've put

you there on a hilltop, on a light stand—shine!
Keep open house; be generous with your lives.
By opening up to others, you'll prompt people
to open up with God, this generous Father in
heaven. (Matthew 5:13-16 MSG)

A couple years after I first read through the New Testament, the U.S. Army came out with their "Be all that you can be" campaign, and it summed up exactly how I wanted to be as a follower of Jesus.

Do you like the directness of what is being said by Jesus? For me, it removes all doubt about my purpose, and I invite you to indulge me for a quick lesson about salt as we unpack the importance of this verse.

Salt is used in the Bible eleven different ways, and the context in this verse is that salt is a spice. A few thoughts about salt—the chemical composition of salt never changes, salt comes from the inside (why else would we need to shake it out?), and a little salt goes a long way.

When I read this verse, it also makes me think of Thanksgiving, especially since I am our resident mashed potatoes chef. Of all the dishes served, it's a high-impact food and is so easy to make. What I notice is that even though I initially add salt, I can no longer taste it after adding butter, sour cream, cream cheese, and milk. At this point there is a deficit of salt. There's no change in its composition; it is simply diluted.

This verse often makes me think about a spiritual trade deficit of sorts. We are called to be salt and light, to export our influence to those around us. But if we're spending more time receiving than we are giving, we risk becoming more and more influenced by the world and losing our saltiness for God's Kingdom. In short, if we aren't salting the world, the world will make us rot.

I've found that in many cases, gratitude is one of the least used and most powerful gifts we have at our disposal. In the late 1990s, I began a practice of catching others doing something right. As a response, I'd write a note and sometimes attach a book or a gift card, acknowledging the instance of which I was appreciative. Countless times, sometimes dating back decades, I've run into people whom I've sent a thank you. They've told me that it's still on their desk, and often I hear that it's the only form of written appreciation they'd ever received regarding their work.

Unfortunately, many in business tend to only show gratitude to those in positions of authority over them, but I've found it's a powerful tool, and a great way to be salt and light, to acknowledge and appreciate individual people regardless of position, from the ditch digger to the business owner.

I had no intention of implementing anything formal with this process, but it's taken on a life of its own since I first began. Now our office team, project managers, and superintendents are empowered to thank the people we work with, including our contract workers. One requirement is that our team writes a note, regardless of whether a gift is given in the moment, and sends it to their company's owner. We don't just acknowledge our gratitude to the employee; we want their employer to know how much we value their contributions as well. This has become a valuable tool and an incredibly popular way to show others that we appreciate them.

It's important to remember that, though it can begin with one small positive action, being salt and light is not about a single work—it's a way of life. Jesus calls us to be salt and light, but He also says that we are light, and a light needs to be placed properly to shine its brightest. It does no good to only shine when it's comfortable or benefits us—we are made to shine in the darkness.

The next time someone bumps into you, take stock and ask yourself the tough questions. What did you pour out? Did you add value to their life? We are called to be salt and light wherever we go—I encourage you to live your lives in a way that will draw people to you and ultimately point them to God.

Takeaways

1. Everyone can have influence. Determine what type of influence you want to have on those around you.

2. A small act of gratitude goes a long way and empowers others.

3. Consistently appreciate and acknowledge those around you regardless of their position.

4. Be salty! Regardless of what culture says, live a life in which your character displays truth and righteousness.

Reflections

1. How can you be salt and light to your leaders and your team?

2. How can you encourage your team and leaders to shine brightly for the benefit of those around them?

3. How can you add additional value (above and beyond your obligation) to your clients or the people you serve?

13

What About Judas?

You may be wondering how I've spent a whole book on the importance of praying over, choosing, and empowering the right leaders for your team without mentioning the elephant in the room: Judas Iscariot.

I'll start by saying, no, Jesus was not surprised by Judas's betrayal. He was intentional about choosing Judas as one of His apostles, knowing beforehand that He'd be betrayed. Judas selling out Jesus for thirty pieces of silver was an important part of the Gospel story from the beginning.

Eleven of the twelve apostles were from Galilee, while Judas Iscariot was from Kerioth of Judea. He was born and raised in the rugged territory where mighty King David learned to become Israel's greatest shepherd and was likely the only selection that would have made sense to the onlookers of his day. But he was an outsider amongst the apostles.

From Judas's perspective, Jesus was a popular and charismatic leader who attracted large crowds, which could have led to more political power, influence, and wealth. "If I hitch my wagon to Jesus," I imagine Him saying, "this will put me on the fast track to success!" While he had the right pedigree and came from the right area, he most certainly did not have the right stuff.

I'm not saying that actively bringing members of questionable character onto your team is something to be modeled. As leaders, Judas's story is a tale that we should learn from. How do we respond when our expectations aren't met, when we are disappointed, or when we are betrayed by those we trust? (At some point, it's bound to happen!)

To be certain, if Jesus was betrayed, we are all at risk. Betrayal comes at different times and situations, and, unfortunately, it wasn't difficult to come up with a list in my own life that's longer than I care to admit.

We had been remodeling for many years and had the opportunity to competitively bid on a new home in Paradise Valley, Arizona. Desert Star was the low bidder, and my dad and I were excited to have the opportunity on this project. The qualification process to get on the list was very involved. The client wanted personal and professional references, and he even wanted to talk to our pastor. He was performing due diligence and wanted to know about our character and integrity.

A short time passed, and we were contacted. The client said that one of the other bidders contacted him and offered to beat our bid price, and he was going to use them and not us. To say we were disappointed would be an understatement.

What happened next? My dad called him a few days later and confronted him, reminding him of our prequalification process and that he asked to speak with our pastor. My dad asked him if he was a believer, and he answered that he was. My dad told him what he did was unethical and quoted Isaiah 54:17, "No weapon formed against me shall prosper." We ended up with the contract amount for our bid. I guess it pays to go Old Testament sometimes!

Unfortunately, there have been many other times of disappointment and betrayal. A single mom needs a car, we personally give her $10,000 for a down payment, and she resigns a month later. Let's not forget the employees who stayed long enough to cash their bonus checks and then quit. We have had a lot of things happen, but our guiding principle is that we choose how to respond in every situation. Do we get bitter, or do we get better?

As leaders, we are sometimes the last to realize when action is required. My friend and mentor Darren Hardy asked,

"When do you fire someone?" The answer? As soon as you think of it.

There have been times when I have kept people on too long because I was unsure what to do or how it would impact the team. The right choice would have been to face the demands of reality. I didn't, and it negatively impacted our team. I apologized to my team and took responsibility for what happened, learning another lesson the hard way.

How did this happen? How were they selected? We should look at our individual selection processes. Look beyond the obvious choices. Make the best decision you can at the time with available information and then manage the decision. Stay engaged in relationships and be aware when changes are taking place. Discern how your response will impact individuals and your team and aim for the response that will make the greatest positive impact.

Is betrayal avoidable? I wish it were, but I am doubtful because we live and work in a fallen world. I've found ways to significantly limit or avoid it in certain areas. Keep your integrity intact and deal with the hard things first. Never keep people for your convenience and hurt your team organization. When you offer something to someone, and they want to change what you intended, do your best not to waver. Questioning the process is fine, but your vision and values should remain unchanged. Be prepared to make the tough decisions sooner rather than later. (As the Chairman of Goodrich Aerospace told me, "Unlike fine wine, bad news does not get better with time.")

Remember that everyone makes daily choices that shape who they become over time. Be actively engaged to see what is going on in the lives of your team members. Keep communication open. Be willing to ask questions (sometimes the hard ones). Also know that sometimes we do the best that we can, but we can't control the choices people make that take them down a different path. Let them go. Stay the course that you were destined for, knowing that not everyone will go the full distance with you.

Takeaways

1. Stay true to your vision and values/maintain your integrity, especially through seasons of hardship.

2. Keep an active eye on your team members, whether it is through a daily or weekly check in.

3. Invest in your team members to the best of your ability but be open to those who choose a different path.

Reflections

1. As a leader, facing betrayal and disappointment are likely inevitable. How can you prepare in advance to respond in a healthy way?

2. What steps can you take to ensure the ongoing health of your team?

3. How can you protect your team from the fallout of a betrayal?

Acknowledgements

To God, the Master Builder, and His Son, Jesus, who invested in building all future leaders and leadership teams.

Thank you to my amazing, loving, supportive best friend and wife of forty years, Carol. You have supported and encouraged me every step of the way. You truly are a "maximizer," and I am thankful you use your gifts with me. Thanks also to my parents, who always encouraged and challenged me—you are both overcomers and firm in your faith. To our sons, Jeremy, and Jonathan, you both inspire and challenge me to become better. To my sister, Sara, and her husband, Joe Mihaljevich, you have been with us through every season of life both as family and best friends.

Thank you to my pastor friends, Lee Domingue, Jentezen Franklin, and Chris Hodges for your leadership and encouragement, and for my many pastor friends and their staff across the country—you have inspired me.

Thanks are also due to Dave Cavan, my dear friend who believes in me more than I believe in myself. Thank you to all of our clients throughout the years that believed in me and our team. You have mentored me in immeasurable ways.

The team at Desert Star Construction and Desert Star Concierge—thank you for who you are, who you continue to become, and all that you do. Neither Desert Star nor this book would be possible without you.

To my editor, Andrew McNamara, you challenged me and drew out more than I thought possible. Thank you for sharing your gift and talent. To Jordyn Scheske, thank you for sharing your creativity and talent in designing the cover for this book.

References

While writing this book, a number of resources inspired and informed my writing. Of particular note is the Olive Tree Bible app and the numerous resources available through the software:

- *For Everyone Commentary Series*
- *The MacArthur Bible Handbook*
- *The Message Bible*
- *Preach the Word* (Stephen Oliver Stout)
- *Preacher Commentary Series*

I also found great encouragement and fresh insights through Matthew Henry's *Concise Commentary on the Whole Bible*, the *Maxwell Leadership Bible (3rd Edition)*, Charles Swindoll's *Insights on Matthew* and *Insights on Luke (Swindoll's Living Insights New Testament Commentary Books 1 and 3)*, and *The Blackaby Study Bible (NKJV)*.

Suggested Reading

While You Wait

What will you do in the waiting?

We've all found ourselves between where we are and where we want to be. That's why the message of *While You Wait* is crucial—the decisions we make today will determine what kind of lives we live tomorrow. What matters to God is not just that we wait but how we wait.

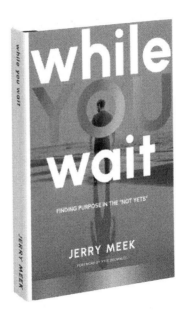

Do we spend our time fearful and anxious, pursuing everything we think is urgent and nothing truly important? Or do we press into God, allow him to grow our character, and learn from whatever season of waiting we find ourselves in? What happens if we invite God to refine and prepare us as we experience His timing?

In *While You Wait*, Jerry Meek, the CEO and Founder of Desert Star Construction and Glorious Reflections, helps us recognize that our obstacles in the waiting are opportunities: opportunities for a more significant victory, greater freedom, a higher purpose, and ultimately a more extraordinary relationship with God. Together we will focus on the magnitude of our God, not the size of our struggles.

Be Great... Before It's Too Late

It doesn't matter whether you are eight or eighty-eight—ordinary can become extraordinary with just a little extra effort, thought, planning, and perspective. In life, we have many opportunities to win or to lose. We are faced with a constant choice: we can become more or we can remain the same.

Are you living a life on its way to being great or a life that will fall short of your ultimate destiny?

In *Be Great...Before It's Too Late,* Jerry dives deep into the stories of some of the most inspiring men and women in history and explores their valleys and their peaks. You will see the benefits of their discipline and the rewards of finishing the race, and you will be reminded of the importance of beginning with purpose and finishing strong.

This book is an invitation to a journey to discover what a life of greatness could look like. While you still have time and a future to experience, what can make the difference in your own life so that you can discover and experience a life of greatness?

Team Builder Toolbox

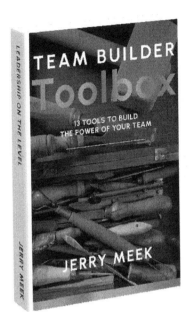

Your team's greatest successes are built with a powerful set of tools. Like a builder's toolbox, these important tools can be collected and shared. Each one has its unique purpose from sharpening leadership skills and refining character to invigorating creativity and advancing personal and professional integrity.

In *Team Builder Toolbox*, Jerry outlines thirteen tools your business needs. These tools were carefully crafted and implemented over time with the same enduring standard of excellence that has been used to build some of the world's most distinguished residential and commercial projects. From the moment you discover these tools for yourself, your best results will connect with your hopes and dreams as they lay the foundation of what you and your team build together today and for the future.

Join the Glorious Reflections Community

Glorious Reflections helps overwhelmed marketplace leaders rediscover their eternal purpose and earthly mission. Led by Jerry Meek, the community is a collective of leaders who desire to live and lead in a way that reflects the glory of God. Jerry is a leader who has been in your shoes and has seen firsthand the power of living a life totally surrendered to God. He is now devoted to helping others do the same.

When we understand that the most authentic person we can be and the most impactful work we can do is found in the One we reflect, we are empowered to live a life of perspective and purpose.

You are invited to join us on the journey so you, too, can live and lead in a way that reflects all of who He is and who you've been created to be.

Sign Up to Join the Community

Take the Challenge: 21 Days to Living and Leading in a Way That Reflects the Glory of God

Some people are talented—they're great at doing something but they're not great at being someone. As a leader, are you making decisions out of your own strength on an empty tank? Or are you seeking God first in prayer, gaining His perspective, and making decisions that best align with His purpose for your life? This 21-day Reflections Challenge is designed to help you do just that.

Our gift to you—register for this email series and you will receive a downloadable PDF to print and fill out each day of the challenge, along with a daily email to guide you through the reflection process. At the end of 21 days, you will feel more empowered and focused as a leader.

By taking the challenge you will:

- Uncover the role your faith plays in your leadership
- Establish a healthy habit of reflection to start your day
- Gain perspective on the deep meaning and purpose of what your life can truly become

Sign Up to Take the Challenge

About the Author

Jerry Meek is the Founder & CEO of Desert Star Construction, known by clients and industry colleagues as "the best team in the luxury home business," and Glorious Reflections, an online community that helps overwhelmed Christian market-place leaders rediscover their eternal purpose and find unending joy in their life and leadership.

Jerry's last decade has been focused on the continuous growth and expansion of Team DSC®. The results have been published in more than 30 magazines and earned honors such as multiple Gold Nugget Awards, Phoenix Home & Garden Home of the

Year, Southwest Contractor, and NAHB Custom Home of the Year. In 2017, Jerry was the first-ever luxury custom home builder to receive Phoenix Home & Garden's Master of the Southwest, an award program in its 30th year that recognizes the best in design and craftsmanship. Jerry also served as the founding president of the Phoenix Dream Center Foundation, which aids young survivors of human trafficking.

Today, Jerry continues to enjoy life's journey with Carol, his wife of over 40 years, in Cave Creek, Arizona, and his adult children, Jeremy (wife, Yasaman) and Jonathan.

You can join Jerry's online community, Glorious Reflections, and follow Jerry on social media by visiting these links:

⊕ jerryrmeek.com | ▣ /jerryrmeek
▣ @jerryrmeek | ▣ /jerryrmeek

Notes

Notes

Notes

Notes

Notes

Notes

Made in the USA
Columbia, SC
05 October 2022